TUTANKHAMUN

TUTANKHAMUN

BY
ROBERT GREEN

A FIRST BOOK

FRANKLIN WATTS
A DIVISION OF GROLIER PUBLISHING
NEW YORK – LONDON – HONG KONG – SYDNEY
DANBURY, CONNECTICUT

For D.R. Green

Cover design by Robin Hoffmann
Cover photograph copyright ©: Art Resource, NY (Erich Lessing)
Map by MacArt Design
Photographs copyright ©: Art Resource, NY: frontis, pp. 8 (both Erich Lessing), 13 (Bridge-man), 38 top, 51 (both Scala), 42 (Werner Forman Archives); The Bridgeman Art Library: pp. 11, 16–17, 35, 46; The Bettmann Archive: pp. 18, 54; Boltin Picture Library: p. 22; Archive Photos: p. 25; The Metropolitan Museum of Art: pp. 30 (Harry Burton), 37, 38 bottom, 40 (both photos by Egyptian Expedition); Hulton Deutsch Collection: p. 32; Photo Researchers: p. 43; Sheridan Photo Library: p. 49 (John P. Stevens); University of Pennsylva-nia Museum, Philadelphia: p. 55; Griffith Institute, Ashmolean Museum: p. 57.

Library of Congress Cataloging-in-Publication Data

Green, Robert.
Tutankhamun / by Robert Green.
p.   cm. — (A First book)
Includes bibliographical references and index.
Summary: Tells the story of the discovery of Tutankhamun's tomb by Howard Carter and Lord Carnarvon and the supposed curse connected with it, as well as information on the life and dynasty of the pharaoh.
ISBN 0-531-20233-X (lib. bdg.)—ISBN 0-531-15802-0 (pbk.)
1. Tutankhamun, King of Egypt—Tomb—Juvenile literature.
2. Tutankhamun, King of Egypt—Juvenile literature. 3. Egypt—antiquities—Juvenile literature.   [1. Tutankhamun, King of Egypt—Tomb.
2. Egypt—Antiquities.]   I. Title   II. Series.
DT87.5.G74 1996
932'.014—dc20   *95-46150* CIP AC

CONTENTS

*To speak the name of the dead
is to restore them to life.*

—EGYPTIAN PROVERB

1

Ancient Egyptian civilization has always had an aura of mystery. Remnants from this era—the great pyramids, the Sphinx, the mummified bodies of pharaohs, gold jewelry—are thousands of years old but often very well preserved, giving us a glimpse into a beautiful, eerie, long-dead world.

When Howard Carter and Lord Carnarvon discovered the tomb of the pharaoh Tutankhamun, the dead world of ancient Egypt seemed suddenly to come to life. The tomb was, for the most part, intact. Tutankhamun instantly became the most famous symbol of the mysterious rites, practices, and lifestyles of the ancient Egyptians.

The pyramids Chephren (left) and Cheops at Giza

LIFE ALONG THE NILE

Egypt is an antique land from which sprang a magnificent civilization more than three thousand years before the birth of Christ. It is primarily a desert country, vast and dry, through which runs the Nile River. The Nile gives life to the otherwise uninhabitable lands of Egypt. Even today, 99 percent of all Egyptians live along the Nile's twin banks. The mountainous highlands in the countries to the south of Egypt give birth to the Nile. After twisting north through Egypt, the river's waters break into the many rivulets of the Nile Delta and spill into the Mediterranean Sea.

Until the Aswan Dam blocked the floodwaters of the river in 1968, the Nile flooded annually. When it receded, it left along its banks a dark, fertile soil good for growing crops. When the river flooded more than usual, the crops were abundant and the people prospered. When the river barely overflowed its banks, drought followed, crops withered, and food was scarce.

Traditionally Egypt has been divided into two kingdoms, Upper Egypt in the south and Lower Egypt in the north. The two kingdoms were united under a single pharaoh, or king, as early as 3000 B.C. They have remained united throughout most of Egyptian history. The Nile provides not only the means for agriculture but also a route of transportation. Boats drift north on the prevailing current and sail south with the prevailing winds.

Perhaps the ease of travel on the Nile made the unification of Upper and Lower Egypt inevitable. It certainly made for an active economic life, as tradesmen distributed crops and other goods to the villages along the river. Sailboats, called *feluccas*, bobbed up and down in the gentle currents. Their white triangular sails looked like a string of flags flapping in the warm winds.

SCRIBES TO THE PHARAOH

Although the office of kingship in ancient Egypt was thought to be divine, the pharaoh himself was viewed as a mortal and accessible to the people. He was surrounded by a large number of attendants and court officials of all types. As time went by, the pharaoh and his courtiers became more and more concerned with recording events in Egypt. A professional class of scribes, or writers, arose to perform this task. Few people could read and write in ancient Egypt, so the scribes became a very respected group. Like many professions in ancient Egypt, the knowledge of writing was often passed from father to son. Others with quick minds, however, could also learn to be scribes, escape a life of drudgery, and improve their social position. Along the marshy banks of the Nile grew the papyrus reeds from which the Egyptians made a form of rough paper, also called papyrus. In fact, the word *papyrus* gives us our modern word *paper*.

The scribes wrote on papyrus with a complex form of writing based on characters called hieroglyphs. Each hieroglyph represented a different sound. When strung together, as in a modern

Royal scribe Nebmertuf writes under the protection of the monkey-god Thot. Durable reed paper made from the papyrus plant allowed ancient Egyptians to record the marvels of their civilization and the day-to-day workings of royal government. Use of papyrus as a writing surface spread to Greece and Italy, and was used by the Arabs in Egypt into the eighth and ninth centuries. Then it was gradually replaced by paper made from wood pulp.

sentence, hieroglyphs could convey complex ideas. The Egyptians used hieroglyphic writing until about A.D. 400. After that time, the meaning of hieroglyphs was lost to the world. Travelers in Egypt could see hieroglyphs on the many monuments left by the ancient Egyptians but could not read them.

THE ROSETTA STONE

In 1799, a stone tablet was found at the town of Rosetta near the mouth of the Nile. On it was carved a single message in three types of writing: hieroglyphs, demotic, a later form of Egyptian writing, and ancient Greek. This stone, known as the Rosetta Stone, provided the key needed to unlock the mystery of the

The Rosetta Stone presents the same text written in three different languages: hieroglyphs (the official and literary language of ancient Egypt), demotic (the common spoken language of ancient Egyptians), and ancient Greek. The discovery thrilled scholars, who assumed that they could easily translate the hieroglyphic text by comparing it with the Greek. But this project continued to puzzle some of the best minds of Europe, until the brilliant Frenchman Jean-François Champollion formulated a theory that explained the oddities of the ancient symbols.

hieroglyphs. In 1822, by comparing the Greek text to the hieroglyphs, a Frenchman named Jean-François Champollion solved the riddle of the ancient Egyptian language. With the dictionary and grammar of hieroglyphs compiled by Champollion, the many inscriptions found on monuments along the Nile could be translated.

The hieroglyphs told the story of the pharaohs, their deeds, and the great events that happened during their rule. Each pharaoh's name was inscribed in hieroglyphs and surrounded by an oval. This oval represented a rope, which the Egyptians thought would protect the pharaoh's name from harm. The oval-enclosed name of a king is called a *cartouche*. The cartouche was also used as a seal and was stamped on objects that belonged to the pharaoh.

Hieroglyphic inscriptions also tell of the religion of ancient Egypt. Like the Greeks and Romans before the time of Christ, the Egyptians worshiped many gods. The major Egyptian gods—such as the sun god, Ra, the fertility goddess, Isis, and the god of the dead, Osiris—had a central place in Egyptian beliefs and practices. There were also many, many lesser gods.

THREE KINGDOMS

The history of ancient Egypt is divided into three main periods: the Old Kingdom (2575–2134 B.C.), the

Middle Kingdom (2040–1640 B.C.), and the New Kingdom (1550–1070 B.C.). These dates, like many dates in history, are only approximations. In each period the Egyptians enshrined their kings in a different place and manner.

The Egyptians believed in life after death. The afterlife, they thought, must be much like life before death. Therefore, when someone died, the corpse was mummified, or preserved, by embalming, drying, and bandaging. Then it was buried with food, clothing, and other objects for use in the afterlife. The average Egyptian would continue tilling the fields in the afterlife, while the pharaoh would continue his hunting and warring. For the average Egyptian, burial was simple. He or she was buried in the sand with a bit of food and a few simple items, such as tools or extra clothing. The pharaoh, on the other hand, received a much more extravagant burial. The Great Pyramid at Giza, for example, was constructed during the Old Kingdom as a tomb for the body of a pharaoh.

As the Middle Kingdom progressed, the age of the great pyramids passed and the kingdom of Egypt began to weaken. Near the end of the Middle Kingdom, the land was overrun by a foreign people called the Hyksos, who occupied the Nile Delta for more than one hundred years. Before the Hyksos invaded, Egypt did not have much contact with other peoples and therefore did not regularly maintain an army.

The Hyksos demonstrated new technological and military techniques to the Egyptians, however, including uses for horses and wheeled chariots. In the process of driving the Hyksos out, the Egyptians developed plans for expanding their territory. During

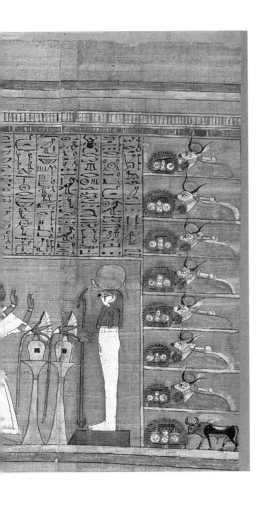

This papyrus from the Book of the Dead *shows the dead cultivating land in the afterlife. The ancient Egyptians believed that the souls of the dead traveled to another world where life continued with many of the activities and concerns of the living. The* Book of the Dead *was believed to provide a guide to magic spells and rites that would protect the soul from dangers in the realm of the dead.*

the New Kingdom they established a standing army, cavalry, and warships. With these forces they expanded south into present-day Sudan and east into the Sinai Peninsula and present-day Israel, Jordan, and Syria. The capital of ancient Egypt had been at

The fertility of the Nile River valley, and its convenient location for trade between East and West, made Egypt a rich prize for invaders. After the Hyksos (also known as the Shepard Kings) conquered Egypt, many other groups also invaded, including the Greeks, Romans, Ottoman Turks, French, and British. But Pharaoh Ramses II, pictured here in a war chariot, led Egypt into a long prosperous period that expanded Egypt's influence southward into Nubia (southern Egypt and northern Sudan).

Thebes since 2160 B.C., a city that was situated on both sides of the Nile. On the east bank of the Nile, the rising sun glittered through the great colonnaded halls of the temples of Karnak and Luxor, which had been built as tributes to the gods. On the west side of the Nile, where the sun sets behind the rugged hills, the pharaohs were laid to rest in an area known as the Valley of the Kings.

The pharaohs had elaborate tombs full of riches of every imaginable shape and variety. These treasures were, of course, a great temptation for ancient robbers, and the tombs were ransacked almost as soon as they were sealed. In the Valley of the Kings, clever robbers burrowed into the underground chambers and took the treasure of kings. Not a single tomb of a pharaoh was found intact until 1922, when the tomb of Tutankhamun was discovered. It was the richest, most breathtaking archaeological find in history.

2

INTO THE VALLEY OF THE KINGS

An archaeologist studies a civilization in the place where it existed. He or she pieces together the past from actual objects left by ancient peoples. Most objects unearthed in an archaeological dig are of interest only to the scholar. But the possibility of finding gold, jewels, and delicate art objects sometimes attracts adventurers and amateurs as well. This is certainly the story of the Valley of the Kings.

The flamboyant American tycoon Theodore Davis was both adventurer and amateur, and most of all he had luck. He began digging in the Valley of the Kings in 1902. Over the next twelve years he hunted down and stumbled across no less than thirty burial sites. Among other finds, Davis discovered objects stamped with the cartouche of the pharaoh Tutankhamun. He found them in a desolate, ransacked tomb. Davis assumed that this little tomb was all that remained of Tutankhamun's burial chamber. He left the Valley of the Kings in 1914. At that time he declared, "I fear that the Valley of the Tombs is now exhausted."

CARTER HAS A HUNCH

Howard Carter, an English archaeologist who had assisted Davis on some of his expeditions, suspected that Davis was mistaken. Carter believed that Tutankhamun's tomb was still in the Valley, although there was little evidence to support this belief. By following his hunch, Carter would uncover the first unransacked tomb of a pharaoh. He would find riches beyond description, earn a place among the biggest names in archaeology, and reveal a glimpse into ancient Egypt that would startle the world.

Howard Carter had learned the skills of drawing and illustration from his father and became a fine watercolorist. It was as an artist that he was asked to join an expedition to Egypt, to reproduce the colorful murals that decorated the walls of Egyptian tombs.

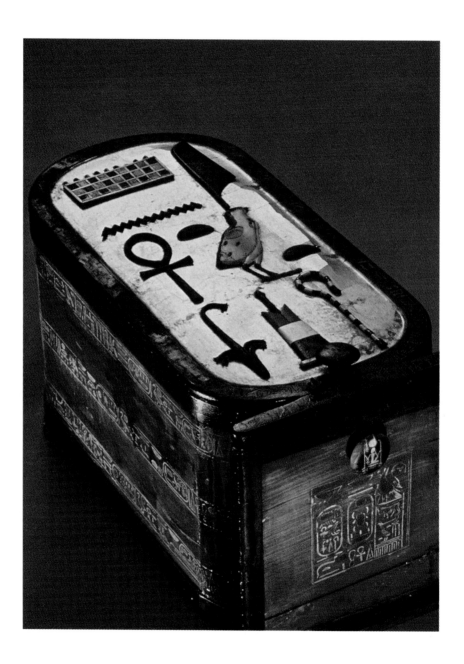

Carter was delighted. He was then seventeen years old. Once in Egypt, Carter soon began to grasp the principles and methods of archaeology.

CARTER'S EARLY CAREER

In 1900, Carter was appointed Chief Inspector of Monuments of Upper Egypt. The Valley of the Kings fell under his jurisdiction, and he became fascinated with the ancient burial site. In 1904 he was transferred to the position of Chief Inspector of Lower Egypt.

The cartouche marked many of the objects belonging to the pharaoh. The oval pattern on the outside represents a length of rope tied at one end. This image symbolized to the ancient Egyptians that the pharaoh ruled all that the sun encircled.

The specific parts of Tutankhamun's cartouche are easy to read: ▬▌ *"Amun,"* 🦃 *"Tut,"* ♀ *"ankh,"*

♀ *"ruler,"* ▮ *"of On" (On was also called Heliopolis, the ancient center of the cult of the sun god Ra),*

⚜ *"of Upper Egypt." Altogether, then, the hieroglyphs read, "Tutankhamun, ruler of Heliopolis in Upper Egypt."*

Shortly afterward he resigned. He was hot-tempered, and many people found it difficult to work with him.

Carter spent the next couple of years doing odd jobs in Egypt, such as giving lectures to tourists, selling his watercolors, buying and selling antiques, and occasionally working at an excavation. It was at this time that Carter assisted Theodore Davis in and around the Valley of the Kings. Then he met an eccentric English aristocrat, Lord Carnarvon.

THE GENTLEMAN ADVENTURER

Lord Carnarvon was a wealthy man who had become interested in the history of ancient Egypt only after arriving there. He was extremely bright but had few strong interests—except automobiles. Cars had recently been invented. They were neither as common nor as fast as they are today, but Lord Carnarvon was intrigued by them and quickly bought his own. Describing himself as an "automobilist," he raced around country lanes in England and Germany. One day, his excitement exceeded his driving skill. He crashed his car and was injured. He was sent to Egypt to rest and recover.

Lord Carnarvon (left)
and Howard Carter

Carnarvon found the search for ancient objects a good sport. Using his connections with the government of Egypt, he was given a permit to dig in Thebes. Every day, clad in a heavy tweed suit, Carnarvon watched his diggers sift the Theban sands. The work went slowly, but a mummified cat was turned up in a cat-shaped wooden coffin. Carnarvon was pleased with his find, which he presented to the Egyptian Museum. That was when he met Carter. The two began a friendly and profitable partnership in which Carter provided the know-how and Carnarvon provided the funds.

TOMBS AND TEMPLES DISCOVERED

Excavations usually went on only in the winter, to avoid the relentless summer heat. In their first five winter seasons together, Carter and Carnarvon uncovered a number of tombs containing the remains of important officials. They also discovered the temples of Queen Hatshepsut (fifteenth century B.C.) and Ramses IV (twelfth century B.C.), and a pair of stone tablets giving some information about the last days of the Hyksos in Egypt.

In 1914, Carnarvon and Carter took over all digging rights for the Valley of the Kings. Again the team found success, uncovering the tombs of lesser figures and the much plundered royal tomb of Pharaoh Amenophis I (sixteenth century B.C.).

Perhaps the discovery of a royal tomb inspired Carter to begin searching again for Tutankhamun. However, World War I slowed the excavations and separated the partners for some time. It was not until 1917 that Carter could again direct all his energy to the search for the tomb of Tutankhamun.

3

THE TOMB OF TUTANKHAMUN

In 1917, the Valley of the Kings might have resembled the shell-pocked fields of France, in which World War I was raging. The valley was covered with pits, and ditches, and piles of earth. Carter mapped the section where he thought Tutankhamun's tomb most likely lay. He began clearing it yard by yard, right down to the bedrock. Carter was patient and methodical in his approach. He was determined not to miss the tomb by chance.

In one corner of the mapped area, diggers unearthed the foundations of huts probably used by workmen in the time of Ramses VI (twelfth century B.C.). Carter wanted to excavate the area beneath the huts. But this would have blocked the entrance to the tomb of Ramses VI, just a few yards from the spot. It was the height of the tourist season, and the tomb of Ramses VI was a popular attraction. Carter usually had little sympathy for the desires of tourists, but this time he ordered the diggers to another area. The diggers would not return to the huts until five discouraging seasons had passed.

DIGGING UNDER PRESSURE

Between the end of the fifth season and the beginning of the sixth, trouble descended upon the Valley. Lord Carnarvon was disappointed by the lack of progress and was suffering from poor health. He informed Carter that he was withdrawing his support for the expedition. In order to save the partnership, Carter offered to pay for the sixth season with his own funds. Carnarvon was so impressed that he changed his mind and agreed to pay for one final season. For Carter, time was running out.

So it was in desperation that Carter returned to the Valley of the Kings in 1922. To cheer himself up he bought a yellow canary, which lived in his house at the excavation site. The bird turned out to be popular with the Egyptian workers. It was nicknamed the "Golden Bird" and became a mascot for the expedition.

Finally, the excavation returned to the area of the

huts in front of the tomb of Ramses VI. The diggers cleared the top layer of soil and removed the huts' foundations. When Carter arrived at the excavation site on the morning of November 4, 1922, the usually talkative workers fell silent. A single step, cut in the rock beneath the first hut, had been discovered. Carter gazed at it with amazement.

Over the next few days, excitement raced through the Valley as the workers cleared one step after another. Carter wondered if this could be the entrance to the tomb for which he had searched for six frustrating years. One step followed another until the twelfth of sixteen steps was uncovered. Then a door became visible. On the door Carter found the seal of the royal burial grounds of Thebes.

Unable to resist a peek inside, Carter carved a small hole into the top corner of the door. By the light of his flashlight, he saw a passageway filled with rubble. To Carter this was proof that the tomb builders

The splendid pyramids provided easy pickings for tomb robbers. Later pharaohs, hoping to foil treasure hunters, had their tombs sunk into the ground in the Valley of the Kings. This picture of the Valley shows the entrance to the tombs of (A) Tutankhamun and (B) Ramses VI.

had gone to great lengths to protect whatever lay beyond the passage.

In an extraordinary act of self-control, Carter resealed the tomb's entrance, filling the entire set of steps with dirt. He cabled Lord Carnarvon: "At last have made wonderful discovery in Valley: a magnificent tomb with seals intact; re-covered same for your arrival. Congratulations."

NEWS OF TUTANKHAMUN GETS OUT

Word of the discovery was cabled all over the world. Tourists and newspaper agents flocked to the Valley. There was the possibility, of course, that the tomb would be empty. The air was thick with tension. Carter's canary, the Golden Bird that some believed had brought such luck to the expedition, was gobbled down by a cobra just days before the opening. The

Arthur "Pecky" Callender and an Egyptian assistant watch with anticipation as Howard Carter carefully unlocks and swings open the gold-plated shrines that encase the mummified remains of Tutankhamun. Callender, who was trained as an architect and engineer, helped Carter extract many of the larger objects from the cramped tomb.

cobra adorns the crowns and burial masks of the Egyptian pharaohs, and, it was believed, protects the pharaoh against his enemies. The death of Carter's pet canary was proof to some of the Egyptian workers that Tutankhamun was angered by the excavation.

When the steps of the tomb were cleared for a second time, the outer door was fully revealed. On it Carter discovered the seal of Tutankhamun. Had he dug just a little farther two weeks earlier, he might have rested easier knowing that the tomb belonged to Tutankhamun. A full view of the door revealed more disturbing news, however. It became clear that the tomb had been entered and resealed at least twice, probably by thieves, and definitely in ancient times.

It took two days of burrowing through the rubble-strewn passageway before a second door was struck. The second door, some thirty feet beyond the first, bore the seal of Tutankhamun and the seal of the royal burial grounds. It also had a small resealed opening through which ancient thieves had passed. Carter, Carnarvon, Carnarvon's daughter Lady Evelyn Herbert, and a few others descended into the passage to force open the inner door. Their hopes and dreams would be fulfilled or destroyed by what lay just inches away on the other side. Again Carter bore a small hole, to which he raised a flickering candle. An uneasy silence fell on the passage as Carter, motionless, gazed through the hole. Finally, unable to stand the suspense, Carnarvon broke the silence: "Can you see anything?"

"Yes, wonderful things," Carter whispered in a shaky voice. He later wrote: "As my eyes grew accustomed to the light, details of the room within emerged slowly from the mist, strange animals, statues of gold—everywhere the glint of gold."

Carter was looking at the first room of the four-room tomb of Pharaoh Tutankhamun. This first room is known as the antechamber. The floor of the antechamber was covered with heaps of trea-

Tutankhamun as the god Horus prepares to spear a hippopotamus. This statue and another just like it were found in one of the twenty-two wooden shrines in the inner-most room of Tutankhamun's tomb, the treasury room.

sure: the king's throne, gilt furniture in the shape of strange animals, silver trumpets, piles of linen cloth, ornate boxes, and overturned chariots. The tomb robbers who had entered thousands of years earlier had left quite a mess. The tomb had been resealed, however, by priests of the Valley. A small hole, probably left by the robbers, was discovered. Carter had visions of room after room full of treasure.

INSIDE THE TOMB

In fact, the tomb had four treasure-strewn rooms. The small hole beneath a couch in the antechamber led to another room full of wonderful objects. Guarding one wall of the antechamber were two life-size statues of Tutankhamun that faced each other across a bare wall marked with royal cartouches. As Carter carefully chipped away at the wall, a golden wall behind emerged. It was one of the sides of Tutankhamun's outermost golden shrine, which nearly filled the burial chamber. Carter drew back the bolt and opened the golden doors of the outer shrine. Inside, with burial seals intact, was another golden shrine. This was the final proof that the king was entombed within, undisturbed for 3,245 years.

The body of Tutankhamun rested in a bewildering series of cases. The four golden shrines encased a giant quartzite sarcophagus. The sarcophagus en-

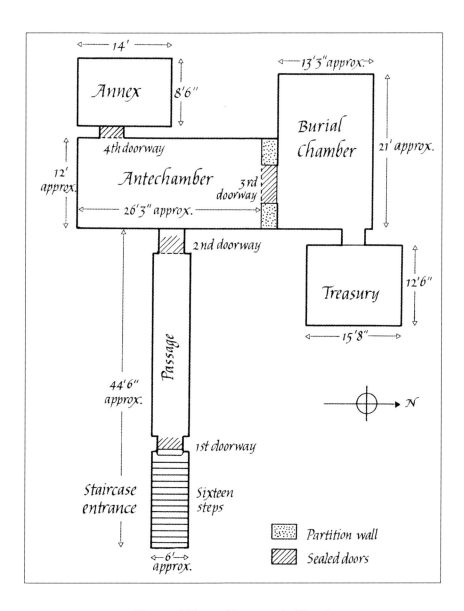

14'

Annex

8'6"

13'3" approx.

Burial
Chamber

21' approx.

4th doorway

12'
approx.

Antechamber

3rd
doorway

26'3" approx.

2nd doorway

Treasury

12'6"

15'8"

N

Passage

44'6"
approx.

1st doorway

Staircase
entrance

Sixteen
steps

Partition wall

Sealed doors

6'
approx.

Plan of Tutankhamun's Tomb

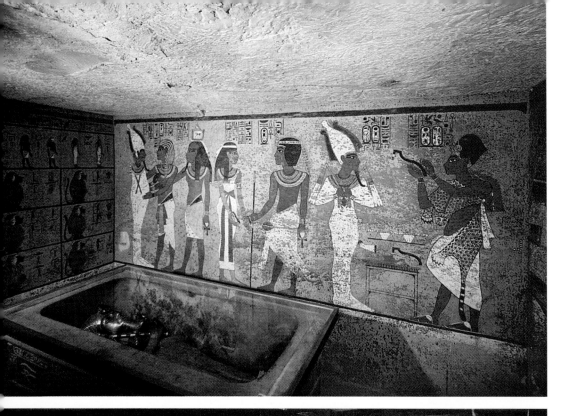

cased two gold-plated coffins and a third, innermost, solid gold coffin. When the final coffin lid was removed, the excavators found themselves staring into a splendid golden burial mask, crafted to resemble the king. The body was wrapped in layer after layer of linen cloth. Many valuable objects were discovered within the mummy's wrappings alone.

Behind the room in which the pharaoh was enshrined was a treasury room. The room contained two stillborn daughters of Tutankhamun as well as the mummified remains of Tutankhamun's organs, which had been removed from the corpse after death in the traditional manner. Carter spent the better part

TOP: After centuries of tomb robbing and the removal of artifacts from tombs by archaeologists, the Egyptian government decided to return some of the mummified remains of the ancient Egyptian kings to their burial places. Though most of the artifacts found in Tutankhamun's tomb reside in the Egyptian Museum, Cairo, the king's splendid golden coffin has been placed back in its original tomb in the Valley of the Kings.

BOTTOM: Howard Carter carefully brushes the dust off the eye of one of Tutankhamun's golden coffins, which lay undisturbed for more than three thousand years.

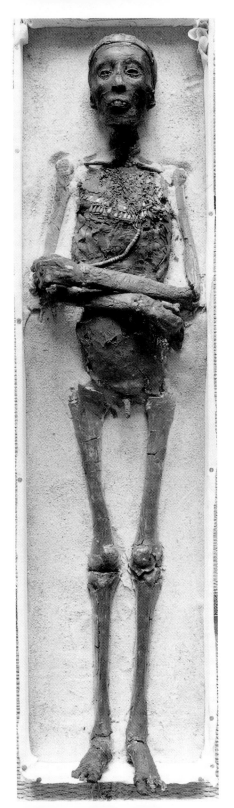

of the next ten years removing the contents of the tomb. He carefully photographed, cataloged, and packed every object. Finally he moved the treasure north on the Nile to Cairo.

Carter accepted offers from around the world for professional assistance. Photographers, botanists, linguists, historians, and jewelers all contributed to the analysis of the tomb's contents. Dr. Douglas E. Derry, professor of anatomy at the Egyptian University in Cairo, and Dr. Saleh Bey Hamdi of Alexandria performed the autopsy. When the last shred of linen wrapping was removed from the head, the excavation team stared in silent wonder at the withered face of an ancient Egyptian king.

The unbandaged corpse of Tutankhamun

4

THE REIGN OF TUTANKHAMUN

Howard Carter once commented that the most important thing about Tutankhamun is that he died and was buried. Though the reign of Tutankhamun was short, to dismiss it as insignificant is a mistake. Tutankhamun lived during a turbulent time in a society that respected stability and permanence.

Surviving records written on temple walls and stone tablets (called *stelae*) tell part of the story of ancient Egypt. Burial tombs, designed to last eternally, tell us even more. Many experts believe that burial tombs reflect the daily conditions in which the buried person lived. If this is true, Tutankhamun indeed lived in splendor. He ruled from a golden throne. On

The back of Tutankhamun's golden throne depicts the queen Ankhesenamun spreading perfumed oil on her husband's shoulder, while the sun reaches toward them with its life-giving rays.

the back of the throne, Tutankhamun and his wife, Ankhesenamun, are portrayed in an affectionate pose. From the many bows and arrows found in the tomb, as well as from the many images of Tutankhamun hunting, we can assume that the pharaoh loved archery. Duck hunting in the marshes along the Nile's banks was a popular sport among ancient Egyptian aristocrats.

The examination of Tutankhamun's corpse revealed the physical characteristics of the pharaoh. Tutankhamun died at about the age of twenty-five. He was about five feet six inches tall. He had a thin nose and full lips, which are realistically portrayed on Tutankhamun's golden burial mask.

The autopsy could not reveal the final mystery of Tutankhamun's life—the cause of his death. No mortal wounds were found on the body. Any remains of poison or disease may have been destroyed by time. Tutankhamun's death remains a puzzle.

Tutankhamun was raised in the court of Akhenaton (pictured here), who worshiped the single god Aton, represented by the sun disk. He moved the capital of Egypt to Tell El-Amarna and attempted to end the traditional polytheistic religion of ancient Egypt. Very few Egyptians actually gave up the old religion, however, and after the death of Akhenaton, monotheism was outlawed.

AN AGE OF HERESY

Tutankhamun was born during the reign of Akhenaton, the most controversial of all Egyptian pharaohs. With Akhenaton's accession to the throne in 1353 B.C., many religious and political traditions in ancient Egypt came to an abrupt end. Even traditional Egyptian art changed dramatically. Akhenaton is remembered as the heretic king for throwing age-old practices to the wind. Once he took the throne, his worship of the sun god, Aton, became his primary passion.

In Akhenaton's religion, Aton, represented by the sun-disk, was fused with Ra, the supreme deity. Akhenaton's devotion to Aton became more and more devout and exclusive, until this one god replaced all the others. At Tell El-Amarna, Akhenaton constructed a magnificent city, painted in brilliant colors. He moved the royal court there and made it Egypt's new capital, replacing Memphis. With its many monuments and temples, the city became a single, vast tribute to Aton. Akhenaton has been called history's first monotheist (believer in one god). Generally, ancient peoples such as the Greeks and the Egyptians held to mythologies, that is, beliefs based on a great number of gods, goddesses, and heroes.

Today the ruins at Tell El-Amarna tell us much about Akhenaton's dreams. El-Amarna was a palace of

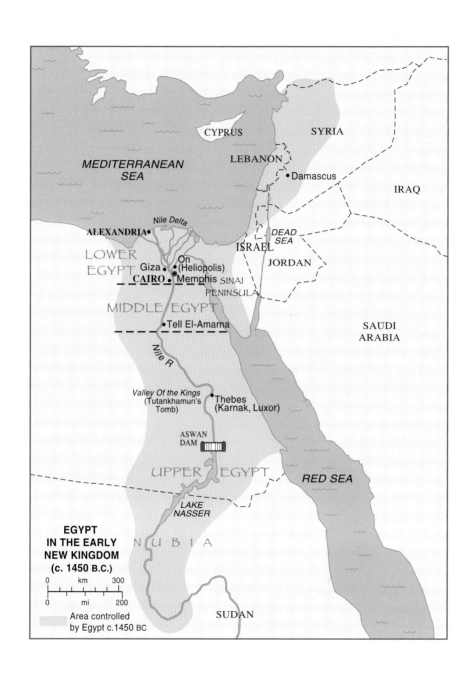

CYPRUS

SYRIA

MEDITERRANEAN
SEA

LEBANON

• Damascus

IRAQ

Nile Delta

ALEXANDRIA•

DEAD
SEA

LOWER
EGYPT

ISRAEL

On
(Heliopolis)

Giza •

JORDAN

CAIRO • Memphis SINAI

PENINSULA

MIDDLE EGYPT

SAUDI
ARABIA

• Tell El-Amarna

Nile R.

Valley Of the Kings
(Tutankhamun's
Tomb)

• Thebes
(Karnak, Luxor)

ASWAN
DAM

UPPER   EGYPT

RED SEA

LAKE
NASSER

**EGYPT
IN THE EARLY
NEW KINGDOM**
(c. 1450 B.C.)

N U B I A

| 0 | km | 300 |
| 0 | mi | 200 |

Area controlled
by Egypt c.1450 BC

SUDAN

Akhenaton and his wife Nefertiti. During Akhenaton's reign, Egyptian art became more experimental and lifelike.

pleasure where the pharaoh lived with his beautiful queen, Nefertiti. He vowed never to leave the city limits of his earthly paradise. Though it is unlikely that he kept his vow, he certainly did let more important affairs fall by the wayside. The vast territories controlled by Egypt were abandoned.

Many statues, wall carvings, and paintings portray the people and events of Akhenaton's time, known as the Amarna Period. Egyptian art generally followed a very steady tradition, characterized by formal poses and expressions and the "idealization" of features. But the works of art that were produced during the Amarna Period are considered to be an aberration from this tradition. This was a time of experimentation and daring creativity. The pharaoh is no longer portrayed as a stiff heroic figure with an angular face. Instead we see a long face with rounded features, and a very human drooping belly. Also, Queen Nefertiti is shown with wide hips and delicate facial expressions. We know that these are innovative artistic expressions, because in the traditional artistic style Egyptians look very similar.

RESTORING THE OLD WAYS

Tutankhamun was most likely the son of Akhenaton and Kiya, one of the king's lesser wives. He grew up in the controversial atmosphere of Akhenaton's capital at Tell El-Amarna and became, like Akhenaton, a worshiper of Aton. We can see many representations of Aton on objects in his burial tomb. However, during his reign, the traditional Egyptian ways were restored. The capital of Egypt was moved back to Memphis, and Amun, the patron god of Thebes, once again became a principal god.

Tutankhamun took the throne in 1333 B.C. at the age of fourteen or fifteen. This was two years after Akhenaton died. A great time of confusion followed the death of Akhenaton. Courtiers, priests, and military figures, angered by Akhenaton's break with tradition, moved quickly to salvage the empire and reestablish traditional ways. The youthful Tutankhamun fell under the guidance of two principal figures, Ay, who would become pharaoh after Tutankhamun's death, and the military leader Horemheb, who would become pharaoh after the death of Ay.

TAKING CHARGE OF THE KINGDOM

As Tutankhamun matured, he assumed more power. It is difficult to be certain which changes reflected the wishes of Tutankhamun and which reflected those of his powerful advisers. The capital was moved back to Memphis, and Thebes again became the principal religious center. During his reign of eight or nine years, interest in Egypt's territories was

The Temple of Karnak was dedicated to Amun, the god of the ancient city of Thebes. The columns of the great hall of the temple are carved to represent the stalks and blossoms of the lotus plant. The Temple of Karnak is located on the opposite side of the Nile from the Valley of the Kings.

revived. Tutankhamun took at least one trip to the southern lands in Nubia, which supplied gold and spices to Egypt. He also may have visited the outer provinces to the east. Tutankhamun's interest in reinstating the traditional gods almost certainly increased as he grew older and his own ideas for governing developed.

Tutankhamun took only one wife, Ankhesenamun. She was the daughter of Akhenaton and Nefertiti, and therefore Tutankhamun's half-sister. Representations of Tutankhamun and his wife show a happy couple. We know, however, that they had no surviving children and that Ay was next in line for the Egyptian throne.

When Tutankhamun died, Ay made all the arrangements for a splendid royal funeral. He oversaw the entire affair himself, before assuming the throne. With great ceremony, Tutankhamun was buried with the treasures that would be found in 1922. Many of the finest pieces found in the tomb, such as the golden throne, gilded couches, and a gilded bed, are in the Amarna style. It may be that Ay wanted these reminders of Akhenaton's heresy to be sealed eternally with Tutankhamun.

The short-lived pharaoh then quickly faded into obscurity. The location of his tomb was probably forgotten. Aside from the early attempts at robbery, the tomb went unnoticed for more than three thousand

This panel from an ivory box found in Tutankhamun's tomb shows the king hunting fowl while his wife looks on. Hunting birds was a favorite pastime of Egyptian royalty. Bows and arrows were sealed in Tutankhamun's tomb for use in the afterlife.

years. Then the king was seemingly awakened from his sleep by Howard Carter to stun the world with his magnificent treasure.

5

IMMORTALITY

When World War I finally ended in early winter 1918, people all over the world hungered for carefree pleasure and entertainment. The discovery of the tomb of Tutankhamun provided just such a thrill. News reporters swooped down on the Valley of the Kings, and a crowd of admirers of the Carter-Carnarvon team gathered to observe the activity.

With the removal of each object from the tomb, excitement seized the crowd. The cameras of journalists flashed from all directions. This spectacle was captured in the pages of the *London Daily Telegraph:*

> The road leading to the rock-enclosed ravine . . . was packed with vehicles and animals of every con-

ceivable variety. The guides, donkey-boys, sellers of antiquities, and hawkers of lemonade were doing a roaring trade. . . . When the last articles had been removed from the corridor today the newspaper correspondents began a spirited dash across the desert to the banks of the Nile upon donkeys, horses, camels and chariot-like sand-carts in a race to be the first to reach the telegraph offices.

In order to rid the Valley of some of the news reporters, Carter and Carnarvon sold exclusive rights to the story to the *London Times* for a large fee. This decision unleashed the fury of competing newspapers. They accused Carter and Carnarvon of selling out. The accusation was not entirely unfounded. Carnarvon, wanting to make back the cost of years of digging, plotted with Carter to capitalize in every possible way on the discovery. Carnarvon was especially eager to have a movie made about it. Meanwhile, Carter published a scientific account of the discovery in 1923, titled *The Tomb of Tut-ank-Amun*. Both Carter and Carnarvon profited from the sale of photographs of the tomb and its treasures.

A MYSTERIOUS DEATH

Lord Carnarvon died suddenly on April 6, 1923. His death ended plans for a Hollywood movie, and it set

An Egyptian carries a painted wooden mannequin of Tutankhamun out of the tomb into the bright, Egyptian sunlight. The mannequin, according to Carter, was "probably used either for the king's jewelry or robes."

This striking bust of Queen Nefertiti was found in the workshop of the sculptor Thutmose at Tell El-Amarna. Even though Thutmose had not quite finished the queen's bust (note that one eye has not been painted), the sculpture has become a symbol of grace and beauty.

off a flurry of new stories in the media. Rumors spread rapidly of a curse that would bring death to anyone who disturbed the eternal rest of the pharaoh. It was reported that an electrical failure had plunged Cairo into darkness at the precise moment of Carnarvon's death, while in England his dog howled and then dropped dead. This was evidence enough for Arthur Conan Doyle, the creator of the popular Sherlock Holmes stories, to publish an article about the affair, in which he claimed that Carnarvon's death was caused by supernatural forces.

According to the newspapers, Carnarvon was just the first victim of the curse. People connected with the tomb began to drop off in rapid succession. Georges Benedite, the head of the Department of Egyptian Antiquities at the Louvre Museum in Paris, died shortly after Carnarvon. A. C. Mace, a member of the Carnarvon-Carter expedition, died shortly after Benedite.

Most of the expedition members, including Carter, lived to an old age, so the press began to

Media coverage was intended to be scientific and accurate, but the mystery of the beautiful objects led many to believe that magic curses protected Tutankhamun's tomb.

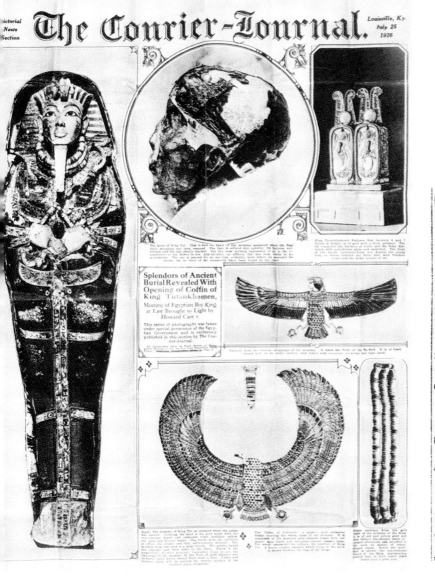

Splendors of Ancient Burial Revealed With Opening of Coffin of King Tutankhamen.

Mummy of Egyptian Boy King at Last Brought to Light by Howard Cart r.

This series of photographs was taken under special permission of the Egyptian Government and is exclusively published in this section by The Courier-Journal.

GOLD-CASED MUMMY OF TUT-ANKH-AMEN IS FOUND IN COFFIN

Opening of the Sarcophagus Reveals Pharaoh as He Was Laid to Rest 3,300 Years Ago.

SPECTACLE IS DAZZLING

Case Is Colossal in Size and Is a Beautiful and Artistic Likeness of the King.

IT HAS CROWN AND SCEPTRE

Arms Repose Across Its Breast and Faded Wreath of Olive Leaves Still Remains on Its Head.

LUXOR, Egypt, Feb. 12.—The lid of the great stone sarcophagus of Pharaoh blame the pharaoh's curse for the deaths of people only remotely connected with the tomb or with Egypt. When the friend of a tourist who had entered Tutankhamun's tomb was killed by a taxicab in Cairo, the curse was blamed. Lord Westbury, a former secretary to Carter, threw himself out of the window of his seventh-floor apartment in London. He had been a believer in the curse and wrote in his last letter: "I cannot stand the horror any longer and I am going to make my exit." An Egyptian was shot by his wife in London after visiting the tomb. Over twenty deaths of this sort were considered by some to be the revenge of the pharaoh. Fear and excitement electrified the public.

The public hysteria led to speculation that written curses might be found on many Egyptian artifacts. Some United States senators demanded the immediate examination of Egyptian antiquities resting in America's museums. No such written curse was ever found in Tutankhamun's tomb. But even today the legend of the curse cannot be separated from the story of the discovery of Tutankhamun's tomb.

TUTANKHAMUN'S WORLD TOUR

In 1961 the contents of Tutankhamun's tomb were shipped to the United States. During the next twenty years, Tutankhamun's treasure was exhibited in the

United States, Canada, Japan, France, England, the former Soviet Union, and the former West German Republic. Today, nearly the entire collection is displayed in the Egyptian Museum in Cairo. The remains of the pharaoh's body, however, still lie in the original tomb. They are nested within the outermost gilded coffin, which rests in the bottom half of the quartzite sarcophagus. The king and his tomb can be visited in the Valley of the Kings.

The ancient Egyptians believed in nothing so strongly as rebirth and immortality. Whether or not Tutankhamun entered the Egyptian paradise of the dead we shall never know. We are certain, however, that when Lord Carnarvon and Howard Carter gazed upon the beautiful and youthful burial mask of the king Tutankhamun, with its sad and unflinching expression, the pharaoh was, in a sense, reborn. After a sleep of more than three thousand years, Tutankhamun became part of the twentieth century. His immortality is assured for as long as his name is uttered. As the Egyptian proverb says: "To speak the name of the dead is to restore them to life."

TIMELINE

Ancient Egyptian history is divided into Dynastic periods. The three main periods of achievement—Old Kingdom, Middle Kingdom, and New Kingdom—are marked by considerable developments in Egyptian civilization, while the Intermediate periods were times of slower development or relative decline. During most of the Late period and the Graeco-Roman period, Egypt was occupied by foreign invaders.

c. 3000 B.C. **LATE PREDYNASTIC PERIOD**

2920 B.C.–2575 B.C. **EARLY DYNASTIC PERIOD**

2575 B.C.–2134 B.C. **OLD KINGDOM**
–Construction of the pyramids of Snefru, Khufu (Cheops), and Kafre (Chefren) at Giza
–Construction of the Sphinx at Giza

2134 B.C.–2040 B.C. **FIRST INTERMEDIATE PERIOD**

2040 B.C.–1640 B.C. **MIDDLE KINGDOM**
–Trade with Sinai, Syria, Libya, and Nubia increases
–Government divisions established: Upper, Middle, and Lower Egypt

1640 B.C.–1532 B.C. **SECOND INTERMEDIATE PERIOD**
–Hyksos invade and rule from c. 1650 B.C.–1550 B.C.

1550 B.C.–1070 B.C. **NEW KINGDOM**
–Thotmose I becomes first ruler to be buried in Valley of the Kings (1497 B.C.)
–Amenhotep IV takes the name Akhenaten, abandons traditional Egyptian religion for sun worship, moves capital from Thebes to Tell El-Amarna (1361 B.C.)
–Tutankhamun born (1348 B.C.)
–Tutankhamun rules Egypt (1333 B.C.–1323 B.C.)
–Ay rules Egypt (1323 B.C.–1319 B.C.)
–Ramses II, possibly pharaoh of biblical Exodus, rules Egypt for 67 years, fathers more than 100 children, signs peace treaty with Hittites (1290 B.C.–1224 B.C.)

1070 B.C.–712 B.C. **THIRD INTERMEDIATE PERIOD**

712 B.C.–332 B.C. **LATE PERIOD**
–Persians invade Egypt (525 B.C.)

332 B.C.–A.D. 395 **GRAECO-ROMAN PERIOD**
–Alexander the Great conquers Egypt, founds city of Alexandria (332 B.C.)
–Cleopatra VII rules Egypt (51 B.C.–30 B.C.)
–Egypt becomes a Roman province (30 B.C.)

FOR MORE INFORMATION

FOR FURTHER READING

Asimov, Isaac. *The Egyptians*. Boston: Houghton Mifflin, 1967.

Harris, Nathaniel. *Mummies*. New York: Franklin Watts, 1995.

Woods, Geraldine. *Science in Ancient Egypt*. New York: Franklin Watts, 1988.

FICTION

Morrison, Lucile. *The Lost Queen of Egypt*. New York: Lippincott, 1937. A historical novel about Ankhesenamun, the daughter of Akhenaton and wife of Tutankhamun.

HOWARD CARTER'S VOICE

BBC 1922–1972. Fifty Years of the BBC. Long-playing double record. BBC, 1972. Includes cut of Howard Carter talking about the discovery of Tutankhamun's tomb.

FOR ADVANCED READERS

Budge, Sir Ernest A. Wallis. *Tutankhamen: Amenism, Atenism and Egyptian Monotheism*. Salem, NH: Ayer Company, 1989.

Carter, Howard, and A. C. Mace. *The Discovery of the Tomb of Tutankhamen*. New York: Dover, 1977.

Reeves, Nicholas. *The Complete Tutankhamun*. London: Thames and Hudson, 1990.

INTERNET SITES

Home pages and directories will link you to a myriad of Web sites about the ancient world:

Exploring Ancient World Cultures (University of Evansville):
   http://cedar.evansville.edu/~wcweb/wc101/
ArchNet (University of Connecticut):
   http://spirit.lib.uconn.edu/archaeology.html
The Ancient World Web:
   http://atlantic.evsc.virginia.edu/julia/AncientWorld.html

The sites you can visit include museums that specialize in the ancient world, such as:

The Oriental Institute of The University of Chicago:
   http://www-oi.uchicago.edu/OI/default.html
Institute of Egyptian Art and Archeology:
   http://www.memphis.edu/egypt/main.html
Karanis (excavations in Egypt):
   http://classics.lsa.umich.edu/kelsey/OutKaranis.html

Some sites focus on very specific topics. Just one example is a site devoted to *The Papyrus of Ani (Egyptian Book of the Dead)*:
http://www.sas.upenn.edu/African_Studies/Books/Papyrus_Ani.html

INDEX

Page numbers in *italics* refer to illustrations